THE MODERN TRAVELLER

THE MODERN TRAVELLER

BY

HILAIRE BELLOC

GYAN

ISBN : 978-81-212-1792-7(HB)

First Published,1898

Published, 2018

Published by

Gyan Publishing House
5, Ansari Road
Daryaganj, New Delhi-110002
Phone: 011-47034999, 9811692060
www.gyanbooks.com
E-mail: books@gyanbooks.com

GYAN

Printed at: G. Print Process, Delhi.

THE MODERN TRAVELLER.

I.

The *Daily Menace*, I presume?
Forgive the litter in the room.
I can't explain to you
How out of place a man like me
Would be without the things you see,—
The Shields and Assegais and odds
And ends of little savage gods.
Be seated; take a pew.
(Excuse the phrase. I'm rather rough,
And—pardon me!—but have you got
A pencil? I've another here:
The one that you have brought, I fear,
Will not be long enough.)

And so the Public want to hear
About the expedition
From which I recently returned :
Of how the Fetish Tree was burned ;
Of how we struggled to the coast,
And lost our ammunition ;
How we retreated, side by side ;

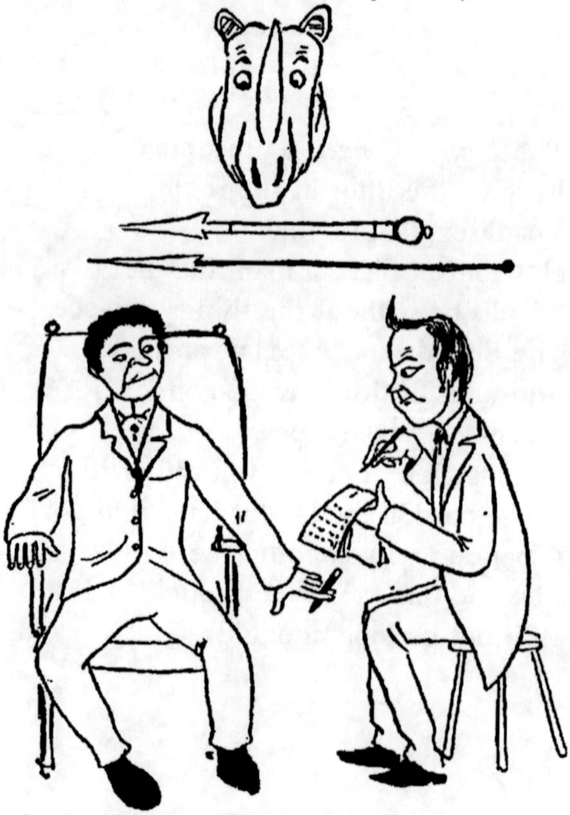

And how, like Englishmen, we died.
Well, as you know, I hate to boast,
And, what is more, I can't abide
A popular position.

I told the Duke the other day
The way I felt about it.
He answered courteously—"Oh!"
An Editor (who had an air
Of what the Dutch call *savoir faire*)
Said, "Mr. Rooter, you are right,
And nobody can doubt it."
The Duchess murmured, "Very true."
Her comments may be brief and few,
But very seldom trite.
Still, representing as you do
A public and a point of view,
I'll give you leave to jot
A few remarks,—a very few,—
But understand that this is not
A formal interview.
And, first of all, I will begin
By talking of Commander Sin.

II.

Poor Henry Sin from quite a child,
I fear, was always rather wild;
But all his faults were due
To something free and unrestrained,
That partly pleased and partly pained
The people whom he knew.
Untaught (for what our times require),
Lazy, and something of a liar,
He had a foolish way

Of always swearing (more or less) ;
And, lastly, let us say
A little slovenly in dress,
A trifle pronc to drunkenness ;

A gambler also to excess,
And never known to pay.
As for his clubs in London, he
Was pilled at ten, expelled from three.
A man Bohemian as could be—
But really vicious ? Oh, no !
When these are mentioned, all is said.
And then—Commander Sin is dead :
De Mortuis cui bono ?

Of course, the Public know I mean
To publish in the winter.
I mention the intention in

Connection with Commander Sin ;
The book is with the Printer.
And here, among the proofs, I find
The very thing I had in mind—

The portrait upon page thirteen.

Pray pause awhile, and mark
The wiry limbs, the vigorous mien,
The tangled hair and dark;
The glance imperative and hot,
That takes a world by storm:
All these are in the plate, but what
You chiefly should observe is
The—Did you say his uniform
Betrayed a foreign service?

Of course, it does! He was not born
In little England! No!
Beyond the Cape, beyond the Horn,
Beyond Fernando Po,
In some far Isle he saw the light
That burns the torrid zone,
But where it lay was never quite
Indubitably known.
Himself inclined to Martinique,
His friends to Farralone.
But why of this discussion speak?
The Globe was all his own!
Oh! surely upon such a birth
No petty flag unfurled!
He was a citizen of earth,
A subject of the world!

As for the uniform he bore,
He won it in the recent war
Between Peru and Ecuador,
And thoroughly he earned it.

Alone of all who at the time
Were serving sentences for crime,
Sin, during his incarceration
Had studied works on navigation ;
And when the people learned it,
They promptly let him out of jail,
But on condition he should sail.

It marked an epoch, and you may
Recall the action in
A place called Quaxipotle bay ?
Yes, both the navies ran away ;
And yet, if Ecuador can say
That on the whole she won the day,
The fact is due to Sin.

The Fleet was hardly ten weeks out,
When somebody descried
The enemy. Sin gave a shout,

The Helmsmen put the ship about ;
For, upon either side,
Tactics demanded a retreat.
Due west retired the foreign fleet,
But Sin he steered due east ;
He muttered, "They shall never meet."
And when, towards the close of day,
The foemen were at least
Fifteen or twenty miles away,
He called his cabin-steward aft,
The boldest of his men ;
He grasped them by the hand ; he laughed
A fearless laugh, and then,

"Heaven help the right! Full steam a-head,
Fighting for fighting's sake," he said.

Due west the foe—due east he steered.
Ah, me! the very stokers cheered,
And faces black with coal
And fuzzy with a five days' beard
Popped up, and yelled, and disappeared
Each in its little hole.
Long after they were out of sight,
Long after dark, throughout the night,
Throughout the following day,
He went on fighting all the time!

Not war, perhaps, but how sublime!

Just as he would have stepped ashore,
The President of Ecuador

Came on his quarter deck ;
Embraced him twenty times or more,
And gave him stripes and things galore,

Crosses and medals by the score,
And handed him a cheque,—
And then a little speech he read.

" Of twenty years, your sentence said,
" That you should serve—another week
" (Alas ! it shames me as I speak)
" Was owing when you quitted.
" In recognition of your nerve,
" It gives me pleasure to observe
" The time you still had got to serve
" Is totally remitted.

" Instead of which these friends of mine "—
(And here he pointed to a line

Of Colonels on the Quay)—

"Have changed your sentence to a fine
"Made payable to me.
"No—do not thank me—not a word!
"I am very glad to say
"This little cheque is quite a third
"Of what you have to pay."

The crew they cheered and cheered again,
The simple-loyal-hearted men!

Such deeds could never fail to be
Renowned throughout the west.
It was our cousins over sea
That loved the Sailor best,—
Our Anglo-Saxon kith and kin,
They doted on Commander Sin,
And gave him a tremendous feast
The week before we started.
O'Hooligan, and Vonderbeast,
And Nicolazzi, and the rest,
Were simply broken-hearted.

They came and ate and cried, "God speed!"
The Bill was very large indeed,
And paid for by an Anglo-Saxon
Who bore the sterling name of Jackson.

On this occasion Sin was seen

Toasting McKinley and the Queen.
The speech was dull, but not an eye,
Not even the champagne was dry.

* Observe the face of William Jackson,
How typical an Anglo-Saxon !

III.

Now William Blood, or, as I still
Affectionately call him, Bill,
Was of a different stamp;
One who, in other ages born
Had turned to strengthen and adorn
The Senate or the Camp.
But Fortune, jealous and austere,
Had marked him for a great career
Of more congenial kind—
A sort of modern Buccaneer,

Commercial and refined.
Like all great men, his chief affairs
Were buying stocks and selling shares.
He occupied his mind
In buying them by day from men
Who needed ready cash, and then
At evening selling them again
To those with whom he dined.

But such a task could never fill
His masterful ambition
That rapid glance, that iron will,
Disdained (and rightfully) to make
A profit here and there, or take
His two per cent. commission.
His soul with nobler stuff was fraught;
The love of country, as it ought,
Haunted his every act and thought.
To that he lent his mighty powers,
To that he gave his waking hours,
Of that he dreamed in troubled sleep,
Till, after many years, the deep
Imperial emotion,
That moves us like a martial strain,
Turned his Napoleonic brain
To company promotion.

He failed, and it was better so:
It made our expedition.
One day (it was a year ago)
He came on foot across the town,

And said his luck was rather down,
And would I lend him half-a-crown ?
I did, but on condition
(Drawn up in proper legal shape,
Witnessed and sealed, and tied with tape,
And costing two pound two),
That, "If within the current year
He made a hundred thousand clear,"
He should accompany me in
A Project I had formed with Sin
To go to Timbuctoo.
Later, we had a tiff because

I introduced another clause,
Of which the general sense is,
That Blood, in the unlikely case
Of this adventure taking place,
Should pay the whole expenses.
Blood swore that he had never read
Or seen the clause. But Blood is dead.

Well, through a curious stroke of luck,
That very afternoon he struck
A new concern, in which,
By industry and honest ways,
He grew (to his eternal praise!)
In something less than sixty days
Inordinately rich.

Let me describe what he became
The day that he succeeded,—
Though, in the searching light that Fame
Has cast on that immortal name,
The task is hardly needed.

The world has very rarely seen
A deeper gulf than stood between
The men who were my friends.
And, speaking frankly, I confess
They never cared to meet, unless
It served their private ends.

Sin loved the bottle, William gold ;
'Twas Blood that bought and Sin that sold,
In all their mutual dealings.
Blood never broke the penal laws ;
Sin did it all the while, because
He had the finer feelings.

Blood had his dreams, but Sin was mad :
While Sin was foolish, Blood was bad,
Sin, though I say it, was a cad.
(And if the word arouses
Some criticism, pray reflect
How twisted was his intellect,
And what a past he had !)
But Blood was exquisitely bred,
And always in the swim,
And people were extremely glad
To ask him to their houses.
Be not too eager to condemn :
It was not he that hunted them,
But they that hunted him.

In this fair world of culture made
For men of his peculiar trade,
Of all the many parts he played,
The part he grew to like the best
Was called "the self-respecting guest."
And for that very reason
He found himself in great request
At parties in the season,

Wherever gentlemen invest,
From Chelsea to Mayfair.
From Lath and Stucco Gate, S.W.,
To 90, Berkeley Square.
The little statesmen in the bud,
The big provincial mayor,
The man that owns a magazine,
The authoress who might have been ;
They always sent a card to Blood,
And Blood was always there.

At every dinner, crush or rout,
A little whirlpool turned about
The form immoveable and stout,
That marked the Millionaire.

Sin (you remember) could not stay
In any club for half a day,
When once his name was listed ;
But Blood belonged to ninty-four,
And would have joined as many more
Had any more existed.
Sin at a single game would lose
A little host of I.O.U's,
And often took the oath absurd
To break the punters or his word
Before it was completed.
Blood was another pair of shoes :
A man of iron, cold and hard,
He very rarely touched a card,

But when he did he cheated.*

* These gentlemen are bulls and bears,
Their club has very curious chairs.

Again the origin of Sin,
Was doubtful and obscure ;
Whereas, the Captain's origin
Was absolutely sure.

A document affirms that he
Was born in 1853
Upon a German ship at sea,
Just off the Grand Canary.
And though the log is rather free
And written too compactly,
We know the weather to a T,
The longitude to a degree,
The latitude exactly,
And every detail is the same ;
We even know his Mother's name.
As to his father's occupation,
Creed, colour, character or nation,
(On which the rumours vary) ;
He said himself concerning it,
With admirably caustic wit,
" I think the Public would much rather
Be sure of me than of my father."

The contrast curiously keen
Their characters could yield
Was most conspicuously seen
Upon the Tented Field.
Was there by chance a native tribe
To cheat, cajole, corrupt, or bribe ?—

In such conditions Sin would burn
To plunge into the fray,
While Blood would run the whole concern
From fifty miles away.

He had, wherever honours vain
Were weighed against material gain
A judgment, practical and sane,
Peculiarly his own.
In this connection let me quote
An interesting anecdote
Not generally known.
Before he sailed he might have been
(If he had thought it paid him)
A military man of note.
Her gracious Majesty the Queen
Would certainly have made him,
In spite of his advancing years,
A Captain of the Volunteers.

A certain Person of the Sort
That has great influence at Court,
Assured him it was so ;
And said, " It simply lies with you
To get this little matter through.
You pay a set of trifling fees
To me—at any time you please——"
Blood stopped him with a " No !"
" This signal favour of the Queen's
Is very burdensome. It means

A smart Review (for all I know),
In which I am supposed to show
    Strategical ability :
And after that tremendous fights
And sleeping out on rainy nights,
    And much responsibility.
Thank you : I have my own position,
I need no parchment or commission,
And everyone who knows my name
Will call me 'Captain' just the same."

There was our leader in a phrase :
A man of strong decisive ways,
    But reticent* and grim.
Though not an Englishman, I own,
Perhaps it never will be known
    What England lost in him !

* This reticence, which some have called hypocrisy
Was but the sign of nature's aristocracy.

IV.

The ship was dropping down the stream,
The Isle of Dogs was just abeam,
        And Sin and Blood and I
Saw Greenwich Hospital go past,
And gave a look—(for them the last)—
        Towards the London sky!
Ah! nowhere have I ever seen
A sky so pure and so serene!

Did we at length, perhaps, regret
        Our strange adventurous lot?
And were our eyes a trifle wet
With tears that we repressed, and yet
        Which started blinding hot?
Perhaps—and yet, I do not know,
For when we came to go below,
        We cheerfully admitted
That though there was a smell of paint
(And though a very just complaint
Had to be lodged against the food),
The cabin furniture was good
        And comfortably fitted.
And even out beyond the Nore
We did not ask to go ashore.

To turn to more congenial topics,
        I said a little while ago
        The food was very much below

The standard needed to prepare
Explorers for the special fare
Which all authorities declare
Is needful in the tropics.
A Frenchman sitting next to us

Rejected the asparagus ;
The turtle soup was often cold,
The ices hot, the omelettes old,
The coffee worse than I can tell ;
And Sin (who had a happy knack
Of rhyming rapidly and well
Like Cyrano de Bergerac)
Said "Quant à moi, je n'aime pas
Du tout ce pâté de foie gras !"
But this fastidious taste
Succeeded in a startling way ;
At Dinner on the following day
They gave us Bloater Paste.
Well—hearty Pioneers and rough
Should not be over nice ;

I think these lines are quite enough,
And hope they will suffice
To make the Caterers observe
The kind of Person whom they serve.——

* * * * * * *

And yet I really must complain
About the Company's Champagne!
This most expensive kind of wine
In England is a matter
Of pride or habit when we dine
(Presumably the latter).
Beneath an equatorial sky

You *must* consume it or you die;

And stern indomitable men
Have told me, time and time again,
"The nuisance of the tropics is
The sheer necessity of fizz."
Consider then the carelessness—
The lack of polish and address,
The villainy in short,
Of serving what explorers think
To be a necessary drink
In bottles holding something less
Than one Imperial quart,
And costing quite a shilling more
Than many grocers charge ashore.

* * * * * * *

At sea the days go slipping past.
Monotonous from first to last—
A trip like any other one
In vessels going south. The sun
Grew higher and more fiery.

We lay and drank, and swore, and played
At Trick-my-neighbour in the shade ;
And you may guess how every sight,
However trivial or slight,
Was noted in my diary.
I have it here—the usual things—
A serpent (not the sort with wings)
Came rising from the sea :

In length (as far as we could guess)
A quarter of a mile or less.
The weather was extremely clear
The creature dangerously near
And plain as it would be.

It had a bifurcated tail,
And in its mouth it held a whale.

Just north, I find, of Cape de Verd
We caught a very curious bird
With horns upon its head ;
And—not, as one might well suppose,
Web-footed or with jointed toes—
But having hoofs instead.
As no one present seemed to know

Its use or name, I let it go.

On June the 7th after dark
A young and very hungry shark
Came climbing up the side.

It ate the Chaplain and the Mate—

But why these incidents relate?
The public must decide,
That nothing in the voyage out
Was worth their bothering about,
Until we saw the coast, which looks
Exactly as it does in books.

V.

Oh ! Africa, mysterious Land !
Surrounded by a lot of sand
And full of grass and trees,
And elephants and Afrikanders,
And politics and Salamanders,

And Germans seeking to annoy,
And horrible rhinoceroi,
And native rum in little kegs,
And savages called Touaregs
(A kind of Soudanese).
And tons of diamonds, and lots
Of nasty, dirty Hottentots,

And coolies coming from the East;
And serpents, seven yards long at least
And lions, that retain
Their vigour, appetites and rage
Intact to an extreme old age,
And never lose their mane.

Far Land of Ophir! Mined for gold
By lordly Solomon of old,
Who sailing northward to Perim
Took all the gold away with him,
And left a lot of holes;
Vacuities that bring despair
To those confiding souls
Who find that they have bought a share
In marvellous horizons, where
The Desert terrible and bare
Interminably rolls.

Great Island! Made to be the bane
Of Mr. Joseph Chamberlain.
Peninsula! Whose smouldering fights
Keep Salisbury awake at nights;
And furnished for a year or so
Such sport to M. Hanotaux.

Vast Continent! Whose cumbrous shape
Runs from Bizerta to the Cape
(Bizerta on the northern shore,
Concerning which, the French, they swore

It never should be fortified,
Wherein that cheerful people lied).

Thou nest of Sultans full of guile,
Embracing Zanzibar the vile
And Egypt, watered by the Nile
(Egypt, which is, as I believe,
The property of the Khedive) :—
Containing in thy many states

Two independent potentates,
And one I may not name.
(Look carefully at number three,
Not independent quite, but he
Is more than what he used to be.)

To thee, dear goal, so long deferred
Like old Æneas—in a word
To Africa we came.

We beached upon a rising tide
At Sasstown on the western side ;
And as we touched the strand
I thought—(I may have been mistook)—
I thought the earth in terror shook
To feel its Conquerors land.

VI.

In getting up our Caravan
We met a most obliging man,
The Lord Chief Justice of Liberia,
And Minister of the Interior ;
Cain Abolition Beecher Boz,
Worked like a Nigger—which he was—
And in a single day

Procured us Porters, Guides, and kit,
And would not take a sou for it
Until we went away.*
We wondered how this fellow made
Himself so readily obeyed,

* But when we went away, we found
A deficit of several pound.

And why the natives were so meek ;
Until by chance we heard him speak,
And then we clearly understood
How great a Power for Social Good
The African can be.
He said with a determined air :
"You are not what your fathers were ;
Liberians, you are Free !
Of course, if you refuse to go—"
And here he made a gesture

so.

He also gave us good advice
Concerning Labour and its Price.
" In dealing wid de Native Scum,
Yo' cannot pick an' choose ;
Yo' hab to promise um a sum
Ob wages, paid in Cloth and Rum.

But, Lordy ! that's a ruse !
Yo' get yo' well on de Adventure,
And change de wages to Indenture."

We did the thing that he projected,
The Caravan grew disaffected,
And Sin and I consulted ;
Blood understood the Native mind.
He said : "We must be firm but kind."
A Mutiny resulted.
I never shall forget the way
That Blood upon this awful day
Preserved us all from death.
He stood upon a little mound,
Cast his lethargic eyes around,
And said beneath his breath :

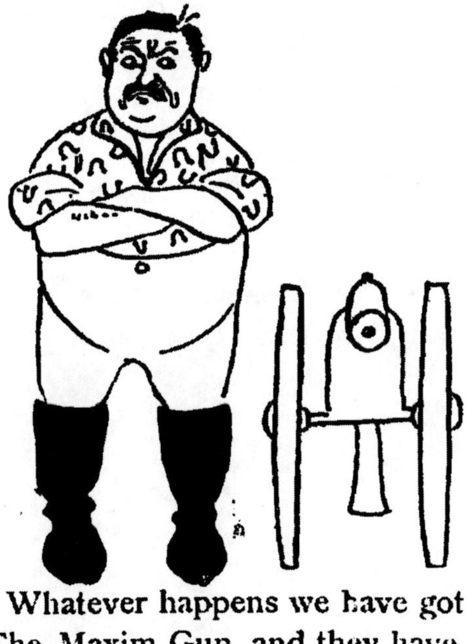

"Whatever happens we have got
The Maxim Gun, and they have not."

He marked them in their rude advance,
He hushed their rebel cheers;
With one extremely vulgar glance
He broke the Mutineers.
(I have a picture in my book
Of how he quelled them with a look.)
We shot and hanged a few, and then
The rest became devoted men.

And here I wish to say a word
Upon the way my heart was stirred
By those pathetic faces.
Surely our simple duty here
Is both imperative and clear;
While they support us, we should lend
Our every effort to defend,
And from a higher point of view
To give the full direction due
To all the native races.
And I, throughout the expedition,

Insisted upon

this position.

VII.

Well, after that we toiled away
At drawing maps, and day by day
Blood made an acurate survey
Of all that seemed to lend
A chance, no matter how remote,
Of letting our financier float
That triumph of Imagination,
"The Libyan Association."
In this the "Negroes' friend"
Was much concerned to show the way
Of making Missionaries pay.

At night our leader and our friend
Would deal in long discourses
Upon this meritorious end,
And how he would arrange it.
"The present way is an abuse
Of Economic Forces ;
They Preach, but they do not Produce.
Observe how I would change it.
I'd have the Missionary lent,
Upon a plot of land,
A sum at twenty-five per cent. ;
And (if I understand
The kind of people I should get)
An ever-present fear of debt
Would make them work like horses,

And form the spur, or motive spring,
In what I call 'developing

The Natural resources';
While people who subscribe will find
Profit and Piety combined."

Imagine how the Mighty Scheme,
The Goal, the Vision, and the Dream
Developed in his hands!
With such a purpose, such a mind
Could easily become inclined
To use the worst of lands!

Thus once we found him standing still,
Enraptured, on a rocky hill ;
Beneath his feet there stank
A swamp immeasurably wide,
Wherein a kind of fœtid tide
Rose rhythmical and sank,
Brackish and pestilent with weeds
And absolutely useless reeds,
It lay ; but nothing daunted
At seeing how it heaved and steamed
He stood triumphant, and he seemed
Like one possessed or haunted.

With arms that welcome and rejoice,

We heard him gasping, in a voice
By strong emotion rendered harsh :
" That Marsh—that Admirable Marsh ! "
The Tears of Avarice that rise
In purely visionary eyes,
Were rolling down his nose.
He was no longer Blood the Bold,
The Terror of his foes ;
But Blood inflamed with greed of gold.

He saw us, and at once became
The Blood we knew, the very same
Whom we had loved so long.
He looked affectionately sly,
And said, " perhaps you wonder why
My feelings are so strong ?
You only see a swamp, but I——
My friends, I will explain it.
I know some gentlemen in town
Will give me fifty thousand down,
Merely for leave to drain it."

A little later on we found
A piece of gently rolling ground
That showed above the flat.
Such a protuberance or rise
As wearies European eyes.
To common men, like Sin and me
The Eminence appeared to be
As purposeless as that.

Blood saw another meaning there,
He turned with a portentous glare,
And shouted for the Native Name.
The Black interpreter in shame
Replied : "The native name I fear
Is something signifying Mud."
Then, with the gay bravado
That suits your jolly Pioneer,
In his prospectus Captain Blood
Baptized it "Eldorado."
He also said the Summit rose
Majestic with Eternal Snows.

VIII.

Now it behoves me (or behooves)
To give a retrospect that proves
What foresight can achieve,
The kind of thing that (by the way)
Men in our cold agnostic day
Must come from Africa to say,
From England to believe.

Blood had, while yet we were in town,
Said with his intellectual frown :
"Suppose a Rhino knocks you down
And walks upon you like a mat,
Think of the public irritation,
If with an incident like that,
We cannot give an illustration."

Seeing we should be at a loss
To reproduce the scene,
We bought a stuffed rhinocerous,
A Kodak, and a screen.
We fixed a picture. William pressed
A button, and I did the rest.

To those Carnivora that make
An ordinary Person quake
We did not give a care.

The Lion never will attack
A White, if he can get a Black.
And there were such a lot of these
We could afford with perfect ease
            To spare one here and there.
It made us more compact—and then—
It's right to spare one's fellow men.

Of far more consequence to us,
And much more worthy to detain us,
            The very creature that we feared

(I mean the white Rhinoceros,
"*Siste Viator Africanus*")
In all its majesty appeared.

This large, but peevish pachyderm
(To use a scientific term),
Though commonly herbivorous,
Is eminently dangerous.
It may be just the creature's play;
But people who have felt it say
That when he prods you with his horn
You wish you never had been born.

As I was dozing in the sun,
Without a cartridge to my gun,
Upon a sultry day,
Absorbed in somnolescent bliss,
Just such an animal as this
Came charging where I lay.
My only refuge was to fly,
But flight is not for me!*
Blood happened to be standing by,
He darted up a tree
And shouted, "Do your best to try
And fix him with the Human Eye."

Between a person and a beast
(But for the Human Eye at least)
The issue must be clear.

* Besides, I found my foot was caught
In twisted roots that held it taut.

The tension on my nerves increased,
And yet I felt no fear.
Nay, do not praise me—not at all—
Courage is merely physical,
And several people I could name
Would probably have done the same.

I kept my glance extremely firm,
I saw the wretched creature squirm ;
A look of terror over-spread
Its features, and it dropped down dead.
At least, I thought it did,
And foolishly withdrew my gaze,
When (finding it was rid
Of those mysterious piercing rays)
It came to life again.
It jumped into the air, and came
With all its might upon my frame.

(Observe the posture of the hoof.
The wire and black support that look
So artificial in the proof
Will be deleted in the book.)

It did it thirty separate times ;
When, luckily for all these rhymes,
Blood shot the brute—that is to say,
Blood shot, and then it ran away.

IX.

We journeyed on in single file ;
The march proceeded mile on mile
 Monotonous and lonely,
We saw (if I remember right)
The friendly features of a white
 On two occasions only.

The first was when our expedition
Came suddenly on a commission,
 Appointed to determine
Whether the thirteenth parallel
Ran right across a certain well,
Or touched a closely neighbouring tree ;
And whether elephants should be
Exterminated all as " game,"
Or, what is not at all the same,
 Destroyed as common vermin.

To this commission had been sent
Great bigwigs from the Continent,
 And on the English side
Men of such ancient pedigree
As filled the soul of Blood with glee ;
 He started up and cried :—
" I'll go to them at once, and make
These young adventurous spirits take
 A proof of my desire
To use in this concern of ours
Their unsuspected business powers.

The bearers of historic names
Shall rise to something higher
Than haggling over frontier claims,
And they shall find their last estate
Enshrined in my directorate."

In twenty minutes he returned,
His face with righteous anger burned,
And when we asked him what he'd done,
He answered, "They reject us,
I couldn't get a single one,
To come on the prospectus.
Their leader (though he was a Lord)
Stoutly refused to join the board,

And made a silly foreign speech
Which sounded like No Bless Ableech.
I'm used to many kinds of men,
And bore it very well ; but, when
It came to being twitted
On my historic Sporting Shirt,
I own I felt a trifle hurt ;
I took my leave and quitted."

There is another side to this ;
With no desire to prejudice
The version of our leader,
I think I ought to drop a hint
Of what I shall be bound to print,
In justice to the reader.
I followed, keeping out of sight ;
And took in this ingenious way
A sketch that throws a certain light
On *why* the master went away.
No doubt he felt a trifle hurt,
It even may be true to say
They twitted him upon his shirt.
But isn't it a trifle thick
To talk of twitting with a stick ?

Well, let it pass. He acted well.
This species of official swell,
Especially the peer,
Who stoops to a delimitation
With any European nation
Is doomed to disappear.

Blood said, "They pass into the night."
And men like Blood are always right.

THE SECOND shows the full effect
Of ministerial neglect;
Sin, walking out alone in quest
Of Boa-constrictors that infest
The Lagos Hinterland,
Got separated from the rest,
And ran against a band
Of native soldiers led by three—

A Frenchman, an official Prussian,
And what we took to be a Russian—
The very coalition
Who threaten England's power at sea,
And, but for men like Blood and me,
Would drive her navies from the sea,
And hurl her to perdition.

But did my comrade think to flee?
To use his very words—Not he!
He turned with a contemptuous laugh.

Observe him in the photograph.

But still these bureaucrats pursued,
Until they reached the Captain's tent.
They grew astonishingly rude ;
The Russian simply insolent,
Announcing that he had been sent
            Upon a holy mission,
To call for the disarmament
            Of all our expedition.
He said "the miseries of war
Had touched his master to the core";
            It was extremely vexing
To hear him add, " he couldn't stand
This passion for absorbing land ;
            He hoped we weren't annexing."
The German asked with some brutality
To have our names and nationality.
            I had an inspiration,
In words methodical and slow
I gave him this decisive blow :
            " I haven't got a nation."
Perhaps the dodge was rather low,
And yet I wasn't wrong to
Escape the consequences so ;
For, on my soul, I did not know
What nation to belong to.

The German gave a searching look,
And marked me in his little book :—
"The features are a trifle Dutch—
            Perhaps he is a Fenian ;

He may be a Maltese, but much
More probably Armenian."

Blood gave us each a trifling sum
To say that he was deaf and dumb,
And backed the affirmation
By gestures so extremely rum,
They marked him on the writing pad :

" Not only deaf and dumb, but mad."
It saved the situation.
" If such a man as *that* " (said they)
" Is Leader, they can go their way."

X.

Thus, greatly to our ease of mind,
Our foreign foes we left behind ;
But dangers even greater
Were menacing our path instead.
In every book I ever read
Of travels on the Equator,
A plague, mysterious and dread,
Imperils the narrator ;
He always very nearly dies,
But doesn't, which is calm and wise.
Said Sin, the indolent and vague,
" D'you think that we shall get the plague ? "
It followed tragically soon ;
In fording an immense lagoon,
We let our feet get damp.
Next morning I began to sneeze,
The awful enemy, Disease,
Had fallen on the camp !
With Blood the malady would take,

An allotropic form

Of intermittent stomach ache,
While Sin grew over warm ;
Complained of weakness in the knees,
An inability to think,
A strong desire to dose and drink,
　　　　And lie upon his back.
For many a long delirious day,
Each in his individual way,
　　　　Succumbed to the attack.

XI.

Our litters lay upon the ground
With heavy curtains shaded round;
                    The Plague had passed away.
We could not hear a single sound,
                    And wondered as we lay—
"Perhaps the Forest Belt is passed,
And Timbuctoo is reached at last,
The while our faithful porters keep
So still to let their masters sleep."

Poor Blood and I were far too weak
To raise ourselves, or even speak;
                    We lay, content to languish.
When Sin, to make the matter certain,
Put out his head beyond the curtain,
                    And cried in utter anguish:
"This is not Timbuctoo at all,
But just a native Kraal or Crawl;
And, what is more, our Caravan
Has all deserted to a man."

*   *   *   *   *

At evening they returned to bring
Us prisoners to their savage king,
                    Who seemed upon the whole
A man urbane and well inclined;
He said, "You shall not be confined,
                    But left upon parole."

Blood, when he found us both alone,
Lectured in a pedantic tone,
And yet with quaint perfection,
On "Prison Systems I have known."
He said in this connection :—

"The primal process is to lug
A Johnny to the cells—or jug.
Dear Henry will not think me rude,
If—just in passing—I allude
To Quod or Penal Servitude.
Of every form, Parole I take
To be the easiest to break."

On hearing this we ran
To get the guns, and then we laid
An admirable ambuscade,
In which to catch our man.

We hid behind a little knoll,
And waited for our prey
To take his usual morning stroll
Along the fatal-way.
All unsuspecting and alone
He came into the danger zone,
The range of which we knew
To be one furlong and a third,
And then—an incident occurred
Which, I will pledge my sacred word,
Is absolutely true.

Blood took a very careful aim,

And Sin and I did just the same ;
Yet by some strange and potent charm
The King received no kind of harm !
He wore, as it appears,
A little fetish on a thread,

A mumbo-jumbo, painted red,

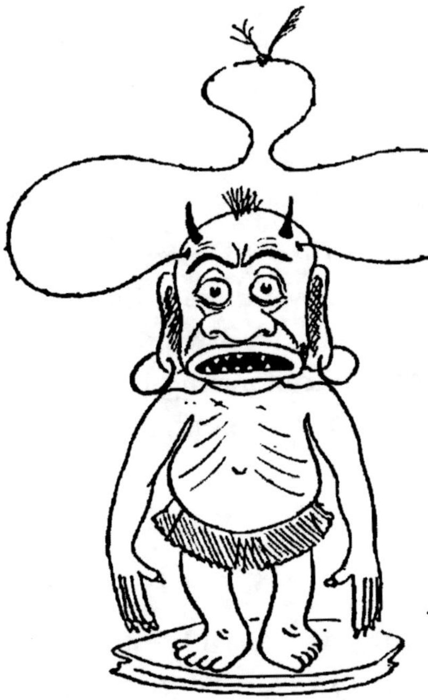

Gross and repulsive in the head,
Especially the ears.

Last year I should have laughed at it,
But now with reverence I admit
That nothing in the world is commoner
Than Andrew Lang's Occult Phenomena.

On getting back to England, I
Described the matter to the Psy-
Chological Committee.

Of course they thanked me very much ;
But said, " We have a thousand such,
        And it would be a pity
To break our standing resolution,
And pay for any contribution."

XII.

The King was terribly put out ;
To hear him call the guard and shout,
        And stamp, and curse, and rave
Was (as the Missionaries say)
A lesson in the Godless way
The heathen will behave.
He sent us to a Prison, made
Of pointed stakes in palisade,

And there for several hours

Our Leader was a mark for bricks,
And eggs and cocoanuts and sticks,
And pussy-cats in showers.
Our former porters seemed to bear
A grudge against the millionaire.

And yet the thing I minded most
Was not the ceaseless teasing
(With which the Captain was engrossed),
Nor being fastened to a post
(Though that was far from pleasing);
But hearing them remark that they
"Looked forward to the following day."

XIII.

At length, when we were left alone,
Sin twisted with a hollow groan,
And bade the Master save
His comrades by some bold device,
From the impending grave.

Said Blood: "I never take advice,
But every man has got his price;
We must maintain the open door,
Yes, even at the cost of war!"
He shifted his position,
And drafted in a little while
A note in diplomatic style
Containing a condition.

"If them that wishes to be told
As how there is a bag of gold,
And where a party hid it;
Mayhap as other parties knows
A thing or two, and there be those
As seen the man
wot hid it."
The Monarch read it through, and wrote
A little sentence most emphatical:
"I think the language of the note
Is strictly speaking not grammatical."

On seeing our acute distress,
The King—I really must confess—
Behaved uncommon handsome ;
He said he would release the three
If only Captain Blood and he
Could settle on a ransom.
And it would clear the situation
To hear his private valuation.

"My value," William Blood began,
"Is ludicrously small.
I think I am the vilest man
That treads this earthly ball ;
My head is weak, my heart is cold,

I'm ugly, vicious, vulgar, old,
Unhealthy, short and fat.

I cannot speak, I cannot work,
I have the temper of a Turk,
And cowardly at that.
Retaining, with your kind permission,
The usual five per cent. commission,
I think that I could do the job
For seventeen or sixteen bob."

The King was irritated, frowned,
And cut him short with, "Goodness Gracious !
Your economics *are* fallacious !
I quite believe you are a wretch,
But things are worth what they will fetch.
I'll put your price at something round,
Say, six-and-thirty thousand pound ?"
But just as Blood began with zest,
To bargain, argue, and protest,
Commander Sin and I
Broke in : "Your Majesty was told
About a certain bag of gold ;
If you will let us try,
We'll find the treasure, for we know
The place to half a yard or so."

Poor William ! The suspense and pain
Had touched the fibre of his brain ;
So far from showing gratitude,
He cried in his delirium : "Oh !
For Heaven's sake don't let them go."

Only a lunatic would take
So singular an attitude,
When loyal comrades for his sake
Had put their very lives at stake.

* * * * *

The King was perfectly content
To let us find it ;—and we went.
But as we left we heard him say,
" If there is half an hour's delay
The Captain will have passed away."

XIV.

Alas ! within a single week
The Messengers despatched to seek
Our hiding-place had found us,
We made an excellent defence
(I use the word in legal sense),
But none the less they bound us.
(Not in the legal sense at all
But with a heavy chain and ball).

With barbarism past belief
They flaunted in our faces
The relics of our noble chief ;
With insolent grimaces,
Raised the historic shirt before
Our eyes, and pointed on the floor

To dog-eared cards and loaded dice ;
It seems they sold him by the slice.
Well, every man has got his price.

The horrors followed thick and fast,
I turned my head to give a last
Farewell to Sin ; but, ah ! too late,
I only saw his horrid fate—
Some savages around a pot
That seemed uncomfortably hot ;
And in the centre of the group

My dear companion making soup.

Then I was pleased to recognize
Two thumbscrews suited to my size,
And I was very glad to see
That they were going to torture me.
I find the torture pays me best,
It simply teems with interest.

They hung me up above the floor
Head downwards by a rope ;
They thrashed me half an hour or more,
They filled my mouth with soap ;
They jobbed me with a pointed pole

To make me lose my self-control,
But they did not succeed.
Till (if it's not too coarse to state)
There happened what I simply hate,
My nose began to bleed.
Then, I admit, I said a word
Which luckily they never heard ;
But in a very little while
My calm and my contemptuous smile
Compelled them to proceed.
They filed my canine teeth to points
And made me bite my tongue.
They racked me till they burst my joints,
And after that they hung
A stone upon my neck that weighed
At least a hundred pounds, and made
Me run like mad for twenty miles,
And climb a lot of lofty stiles.
They tried a dodge that rarely fails,
The tub of Regulus with nails—
The cask is rather rude and flat,
But native casks are all like that—
The nails stuck in for quite an inch,
But did I flinch? I did not flinch.

In tones determined, loud, and strong

I sang a patriotic song,

Thank Heaven it did not last for long!
My misery was past;
My superhuman courage rose
Superior to my savage foes;
They worshipped me at last.
With many heartfelt compliments,
They sent me back at their expense,
And here I am returned to find
The pleasures I had left behind.

To go the London rounds!
To note the quite peculiar air
Of courtesy, and everywhere
The same unfailing public trust
In manuscript that fetches just
A thousand! not of thin Rupees,
Nor Reis (which are Portuguese),
Nor Rubles; but a thousand clear
Of heavy, round, impressive, dear,
Familiar English pounds!

Oh! England, who would leave thy shores—
Excuse me, but I see it bores
A busy journalist
To hear a rhapsody which he
Could write without detaining me,
So I will not insist.
Only permit me once again
To make it clearly understood

That both those honourable men,
Commander Sin and Captain Blood,
Would swear to all that I have said,
Were they alive ;

but they are dead !